T0196762

The Boaz
ENCOUNTER

The Journey to Destiny

Rhonda Amsterdam

authorHOUSE®

AuthorHouse™
1663 Liberty Drive
Bloomington, IN 47403
www.authorhouse.com
Phone: 1-800-839-8640

Published by AuthorHouse 8/16/2013

ISBN: 978-1-4817-7082-8 (sc)
ISBN: 978-1-4817-7081-1 (e)

Library of Congress Control Number: 2013911454

Because of the dynamic nature of the Internet, any web
addresses or links contained in this book may have changed
since publication and may no longer be valid.

APPRECIATION

Heartfelt appreciation is given to my husband and children for the patience they showed while I was writing this book and to Judith Allen for her invaluable contributions.

TABLE OF CONTENTS

The picture we paint with our lives would be the
one we leave hanging in the halls of time.
The choices we make would be reflected in the picture we paint.
Many had graced these halls.
Some have left behind beautiful portraits which have caused
generations as they passed along to stop and stare, to admire
and discuss, to marvel in amazement not just at the gentleness
and sincerity with which they painted their portrait,
but also to ponder on the indescribable simplicity with
which they stepped into a frame designed by destiny and
turned a gloomy picture into an extraordinary portrait.

CHAPTER ONE

Finding Purpose in Tragedy

The Power of Choice

Choice is the most powerful weapon we could ever wield. It can protect us or destroy us. When used wisely this weapon can set us on the path to destiny and when used unwisely it can cause us to encounter destruction. The choices we make today can cause all of our peace of mind to be swallowed up in darkness like yesterday's noon or it can erase all of the pain of our past. Today's choices possess the power to influence all of our tomorrows. God never took the power of choice away from us but granted us the privilege to choose as we wish. In fact, where there is no privilege to exercise choice there is no real opportunity to experience true freedom. Yet, the weapon of choice when not wisely wielded will deprive us of the freedom we so deeply desire. For this reason we must make meaningful choices prayerfully and thoughtfully.

I wrote this book specifically for women but its content is relevant for both women and men. Whilst both women and men may encounter similar situations, the female specie tend to take a longer time to recover from the negative impact of their encounter and are more likely to succumb to the feeling of being powerless.

Moreover, through out our lives we will encounter harsh, undesirable situations which will attempt to rob us of the pleasantness of life and present the façade that we are powerless. But regardless of how dark and dismal the situation may look we can emerge triumphantly if we understand how powerful we are for in us lies the power to make choices inspite of what we go through. I consider choice a weapon since it is a God-given privilege with which we are always armed. The privilege of making choices empowers us to be effective.

For that reason I consider it necessary that we take a closer look at the life of this young woman Ruth. Her story is recorded in a book in the Bible named after her. She entered the pages of the Bible in the midst of what I would consider not only unpleasant circumstances but great tragedy. Yet she was able to conclude the chronicle of her life triumphantly. She completely transformed her life into something beautiful by simply making wise choices and left to hang in the halls of time a beautiful masterpiece, a place for us to gather around, to stare, admire and discuss.

Ruth

> And the servant set over the reapers answered, she is the Moabitish girl who came back with Naomi from the country of Moab. And she said, I pray you, let me glean and gather after the reapers among the sheaves. So she came and has continued from early morning until now, except when she rested a little while in the house.
>
> Ruth 2:6-7

Ruth, a woman of Moab, married into a family who had left their homeland, Israel, in search of a better life. This move was induced by a famine which had devoured the bounty of their land. The head of this family Elimelech accompanied by his wife Naomi and their two sons Mahlon and Chilion, headed for and settled in the Country of Moab. During the course of time Elimelech died. Naomi and her two sons were left to continue their lives. Chilion and Mahlon married two young women of Moab. Chilion was married to Orpah and Mahlon to Ruth. After years of marriage, the undesirable happened; death visited this family again. This time it took both Chilion and Mahlon, leaving three grieving, devastated women shattered and alone.

When we come to the end of ourselves, God will come to rescue us. In the midst of tragedy and grief, Naomi got good news. The Lord had blessed His people by giving them good crops again. So she decided to return home to Israel. Accompanied by her daughters-in-law Orpah and Ruth, Naomi was homeward bound; however, on the way Naomi perhaps realized that she had nothing to offer these two young women. Of course she had good news about God blessing His people with good crops back home. She was returning to her home country, but these two girls were about to become foreigners in a strange land. Naomi desired for them to have a secure future, but had no substance to offer them, nor any guarantee that once they got to Israel life would be good to them. So she told them to return to their mothers' house and she blessed them, Ruth 1:8,9; "And Naomi said to her two daughters-in-law, "Go, return each to her mother's house. The LORD deal kindly with you, as you have dealt with the dead and with me. The LORD grant that you may find rest, each in the house of her husband."

In the aftermath of our negative experiences, like the experiences of these two young women, we also find ourselves presented with suggestions and confronted by choices. We must admit that making choices is not always simple, particularly after experiencing circumstances as difficult as that of Orpah and Ruth. In this saga of Naomi, Orpah and Ruth , Naomi made one suggestion to the two young women accompanying her they however, made completely different choices. Their story records for us that with a little more persuasion from Naomi, Orpah conceded. But Ruth clung to her. Ruth 1:11-14 "But Naomi said Turn back, my daughters, why will you go with me? Have I yet sons in my womb that may become your husbands? Turn back, my daughters, go; for I am too old to have a husband. If I should have a husband tonight and bear sons, would you wait till they are grown? Would you therefore refrain from marrying? No, my daughters. It is more bitter for me than for you, because the Lord had gone out against me".

Those factors that influence our choices would determine whether we encounter triumph or spiral downwards in unchartered dimensions of difficulties. Like Orpah and Ruth our choices are influenced either by practical factors or spiritual enlightenment.

Orpah's choice was influence by Naomi's suggestion. Naomi's suggestion was based on practical factors which gained its strength from the superficial appearances of that which seemed best. Naomi was concerned that she was not at the age to bear more sons to marry these young ladies as her culture allowed. Thus, she was concerned about their future, particularly their future with her, an old woman.

We cannot deny the fact that there are times when it is absolutely necessary that we make choices based on the practical in order to maximize our rewards. However, it is important that we know when to base our choices on the practical and when not to. Oftentimes, people's suggestions as reflected in Naomi's can be based purely on practical factors. Whilst the intent of their hearts is good, their overall view of our future is limited. When we in turn make important choices based only on suggestions made by people with good intention the degree of triumph we experience would be limited. This is reflected in the fact that after Orpah returned to her mother's house we never heard of her again. On the other hand, Ruth's name was fixed amongst some outstanding people. In fact she was one of the few women listed in the genealogy of Jesus Christ.

It is my conviction that although Ruth listened to Naomi, she based her choice not on what she heard but what she felt. This is one of the ways in which God reveals his will for our lives. Whilst we cannot ignore the fact that God will sometimes reveal his will to us through people, as in Ruth's case this was not so. I am convinced that God lead Ruth to make the choice to accompany Naomi. The leading of the Holy Spirit is often presented as an inner tug or that which some people describe as a feeling. Ruth responded to that inner tug, and followed Naomi into destiny.

When presented with the choice to return to her mother's house Ruth was already journeying to Israel. Thus, she did not have the luxury of time to fast and pray about the situation at hand. However, because of her willingness to listen and respond appropriately to that inner thug from God, she immediately knew what she had to do. The Holy Spirit is always there to lead us in the direction that we should take and like Ruth we must be willing to listen and obey. We demonstrate this willingness to follow the leadings of the Holy Spirit through act of faith. Sometimes an act of faith may mean not having the slightest clue why we are doing what we are doing, yet we do it because of the Holy Spirit's leading. When we act in faith and obedience to the Holy Spirit while in the midst of difficult situations, and even after encountering tragedy of any kind, we accentuate our opportunity of emerging triumphantly. Too often we expect great triumph but experience very little change because we refuse to move in the direction which the Holy Spirit in leading as we see no beckoning light flickering at the end of the tunnel. Hebrews

11:6 tells us this *"But without faith it is impossible to please God and be satisfactory to him.* For whoever would come near to God must [necessarily] believe that God exists and that He is the rewarder of those who earnestly *and* diligently seek Him [out]," (emphasis added). James 2:17 backs that up by saying. "So also faith, if it does not have works (deeds and actions of obedience to back it up), by itself is destitute of power (inoperative, dead)."

When we follow the leadings of the Holy Spirit would our choices go unchallenged? No. Our choices would be challenged by opposing opinions, conflicting situations and our contradicting thoughts. Ruth followed that inner tug but her choice was challenged. Once again she was told to go home by the woman she made the decision to stay with. "See," Naomi said to her, "your sister-in-law has gone back to her people and to her gods. You should do the same," Ruth 1:15.

Challenges will weaken those who are not confident in their choices and strengthen those who are confident. Ruth was so resolute in the choice she made that she did not only cling to Naomi but she made a vow to this older woman in verse16 of chapter 1, saying, "I will go wherever you go and live wherever you live. Your people will be my people, and your God will be my God. I will die where you die and I will be buried there. May the Lord punish me severely if I allow anything but death to separate us."

To the person who finds solace in basing their choices on the practical factors, Ruth's choice to accompany Naomi to Israel rather than returning to her mother's house would seem somewhat silly. From a superficial point of view, Ruth was throwing aside the opportunity of returning to her mother's house, a place she was familiar with, a place of comfort and security, and a place from which she could have remarried someone from her nation and start life afresh. Instead she turned her back on the familiar to live amongst people she did not know, in a nation where she had never been. This young woman ignored the fact that she was from a race of people despised by Israel. She was a Moabitess. Moab was one of the nations that had not shown kindness to Israel during their Exodus from Egypt and had oppressed them during the period of the judges. She risked being rejected. A nation at tension with her's, she entered, vowing to accept them and their God. It is most natural to think, "What caused her to make such a decision?"

Recognizing a Destiny Connection

Ruth recognized the role Naomi played in her life. As long as we live, there will be people in our lives, some for a season and others for a lifetime. Some people would be placed in our lives to nurture the sense of purpose   God has placed in us, thus creating the environment for destiny to be birthed, and we would be placed in the lives of others to do likewise. There are those persons who are assigned to prepare us to walk in our destiny, and there are those who will walk with us into our destiny. It would always be up to us to discern why God would have placed in our lives the persons he allowed us to encounter. Being able to differentiate the roles of these individuals is paramount in order to understand and appreciate their inputs in our lives. This knowledge empowers us to make the right choices at the appropriate time. Ruth possessed this knowledge, she recognized Naomi as the person who would walk with her into her destiny. Thus, her destiny was connected with Naomi.

The Encarta Dictionaries define destiny as "Somebody's preordained future". Preordained simply implies that something was "set in advance". Spiritually speaking, God has preordained a good future for everyone he placed on the earth. Jeremiah 29:11

confirms, "For I know the thoughts *and* plans that I have for you, says the Lord, thoughts and plans for welfare *and* peace and not for evil, to give you hope *in your final outcome*", (emphasis added). The Encarta Dictionaries also defines destiny as "Inner realizable purpose of life". This means, whatever God has destined for us to do and become in life, is possible. God, at his appointed time and in his unique way according to his desires reveals to us the preordained, possible to achieve plans he has set for our lives. Our destiny is realized when we make choices to accommodates God's preordained plans for our lives.

Moreover, when we recognize that God would have connected our destiny to our husband, (once we are married our destiny would be connected to our spouse) a person, a place, a church, a ministry, or a job we should earnestly commit ourselves to it, being totally conscious of the fact that our lives and future depend on it. Ruth did not just discern that she should stay with Naomi and cling to her, but Ruth vowed committing herself totally to Naomi. Because of her commitment she accepted Naomi's people and Naomi's God. She was passionate in her persuasion.

In our generation, it is quickly becoming an accepted norm for the power of choice to be misappropriated. Consequently, many of us have come to see possessing the power of choice as doing what is best for the individual known as "me". Inevitably, this mind set is the seed bed for disaster, particularly in adverse situations. Thus, whenever unpleasant circumstances are encountered and choices are to be made in our marriage, ministry, on our job, or other associations, the desire for personal gratification influences the reckless choices of those who are selfish, and acts of fortitude, forgiveness and commitment by those who are selfless are considered as weaknesses.

Traits of a Destiny Connection

The character of the persons we connect ourselves to can positively or negatively impact us as we set out to fulfill destiny. Therefore, it is necessary that we take time to know people before forming close connections with them. A first impression does not always present a solid base for us to build accurate opinion of persons. Taking time to know persons through friendship works to our advantage as knowing someone in a personal way gives us the opportunity to experience their personality traits. There are certain traits which should be resident in a person whom you connect yourself to.

The fruit of love should be evident in his or her life. God is love. The attribute of love in God is evident in his care, kindness, mercy and the good things he gives to us and does for us, Jeremiah 31: 3-4. The love of God is also evident in the thoughts he thinks concerning us, Jeremiah 29:11. Even when God is chastening us he does so out of his heart of love. 1 Corinthians 13:4-7 tells us what love is, therefore, we know what love is not.

They should be selfless. The selflessness of Naomi's heart may have merited Ruth's reasons for clinging to her. Naomi did not try to keep this young woman for personal gain. Perhaps, she saw potential in Ruth. Ruth's youthfulness was in bloom. Naomi was an old woman on a journey home. Sending Ruth away meant taking a long, lonely journey. She could have dragged Ruth along so that she could have company, or to have someone to fetch her bags. Naomi chose to release this young woman to continue her life.

The person you connect yourself to should be able to discern and acknowledge your present level of spiritual maturity and be anointed to propel you to your next level in God. There are spiritual leaders who tend to bundle everyone they lead in the same parcel, ignoring the fact that all do not have the same grace on their lives, all are not at the same level of spiritual maturity and all do not grow at the same pace. Bundling often results in frustration and disagreements. As you grow spiritually it becomes more beneficial to seek someone who is able to mentor. Your mentor should not only be able to discern your present level of spiritual maturity but also determine the pace of your spiritual growth and determine which methods they need to employ so that you may be effectively trained and equipped.

They must be good company. We must not only feel that it is right for us to be with them, but we must feel good about it. The person we connect ourselves to should be caring and should bring out the best in us. When the trait of goodness is present these persons will acknowledge our strengths and challenge us not to see our faults as overwhelming but as small things which we can easily overcome. This trait of goodness will cause these persons to fight our fights with us and be there to celebrate our victories and achievements.

We need to understand that some things God would do for us and some things we must do for ourselves. Therefore, it would always be our responsibility to be mindful of whom we allow in our lives, whom we allow to get close to us, and to whose authority we submit. It is never God's desire for us to draw close, to connect ourselves to people who continually oppresses, mistreats, condemns, and criticizes us and certainly not to those who constantly try to compete with us. None of these things work in the best interest of healthy relationships. And the reality is, we will either honor the privilege or feel the pain of our connections. Therefore, it is always to our advantage that we watch the company we keep. I am not saying that we should look for perfect people. Naomi was not perfect. She had issues.

She was a bitter old woman, who blamed God for her suffering and misfortune, but she was good company.

A Time for Everything

Whenever we think about purpose, destiny and decisions we must also consider timing. To everything there is a season, and a time for every matter or purpose under heaven, Ecclesiastes 3:1. Everything that is set to happen has a set time when it should happen. The same God who designs purpose and assigns destiny also sets the time in which the purpose will come to pass and destiny fulfilled. We could understand purpose and destiny perfectly, and become so driven by it that we disregard timing and throw our lives out of synchronization. Therefore we must exercise patience to wait for our time and season. The Holy Spirit will not just let us know what we should do, but he will let us know when.

Another principle about time and season is that just as no one can manipulate a mango tree to bear cherries so also, no one can manipulate the events of a set time and season for or against us. However timing can be frustrated by our self centered intervention to make a event happen before its set time. Going before God's time means that we go alone and we do things in our own strength. This could mean unnecessary hardship and difficulties and experiences which were meant to be delightful and sweet could be sour and bitter to the taste.

Understanding Purpose

In our greatest tragedy comes our greatest opportunity for us to experience our greatest success or our greatest failure. The way we respond to hardships and difficult situations will determine our experience as a result of these encounters. Life incidentally throws us stuff that we are not prepared for as; disappointments, hard situations, tragic situations, sickness and death.

We will all face tragedy of one kind or another. God will allow us to face such whenever He desires to transition us from our usual place, into our purpose. In the same vein we must also understand that not everything negative that happens to us is as a result of God wanting to bring changes in our lives. Some negative events occur as a result of the bad choices we and those around us sometimes make. Yet we cannot deny the fact that these negatives hold the potential to, more often than not completely impair our ability to clearly see the fine portrait of our lives which God eagerly desires to paint. Holding on to the familiar; the place where we are, who we are or the possession we have, often makes difficult the process of transition. Therefore, as God begins to shift us out of that usual place we become heartbroken as we feel the blunt of adversity because, we do not have the big picture in view.

As a result, we experience; depression, sadness, anger, hurt, shame, bitterness and the list can go on and on. Should these emotions be allowed to take control, they will deceive us into thinking that our destruction is imminent, when in reality God is birthing destiny in us. During this birthing process people will be shifted in and out of our lives. Our protective layer, our normal way of life, will and must be revolutionized so that we could break free into our destiny. This protective layer could mean losing a job, or making serious career choices and changes, losing property or other possessions. It could also mean moving to a new place and learning a new way of life. So whatever face the transition takes is often intimidating and difficult.

The birthing of our destiny is never easy or predictable, it is similar to a woman at child's birth. She has no control over the birth pangs experienced or of the time it would end. Likewise, we have no control over the process of being birthed into destiny. God decides the beginning from the end accordingly as he decides our individual purpose. Our role is to humbly submit to the process. While being birthed God refines us. Philippians 1:6 comfort those who will encounter and endure the birth pangs that unlock their destiny with these words. "And I am convinced *and* sure of this very thing, that He Who began a good work in you will continue until the day of Jesus Christ [right up to the time of His return], developing [that good work] *and* perfecting *and* bringing it to full completion in you". This made Ruth such an outstanding woman. Although she was kissed by tragedy, she committed herself to God, submitted her ways to him through Naomi, and stayed on course during her processing. Throughout the pages of this book we will look at Ruth's journey so that we may be encouraged.

Many persons missed their purpose because they fainted during their time of refining. Although most persons understand and would like to walk in purpose, many do not have enough patience to endure the process. And many lack the faith that being refined requires. This hinges on the fact that many persons do not spend enough time in prayer and the word of God so that they can be empowered, energized and sustained so that they can stay on course. The indisputable fact is this; we will reap the rewards of our choices whether good or bad. If we choose to submit to being refined no matter how long or hard, it will result in us declaring in the end, "...all things work together for good to them that love God, to them who are called according to his purpose," Romans 8:28

This concept of our processing is as a land owner who desires to build a larger building on his property; he firstly designs the new structure he desires to erect in place of the existing one. After which he proceeds to hire contractors to demolish the existing building, to remove the unwanted material and to erect the new structure. During this process the landowner ensures that this new structure is built to specifications.

God has already preplanned our lives, before we were conceived, even before our parents were conceived. He had us in mind before He created the earth. As time unfolds, purpose unfolds. Of course it is never easy to be calm at watching our life fall apart. It is discomforting to feel the cold wind of hardship blowing over our backs in the absence of the comforts we are used to, our protective layer. So whilst being refined we may feel vulnerable, even embarrassed as God removes the debris from our lives. We need to remember, however, that this is necessary. We must take comfort in the fact that whenever God uproots and tears down; it is because He has every intention of rebuilding and replanting. Whenever God rebuilds someone or something it is always bigger and greater than it was before.

This is why we should not become upset with people when God uses them as contractors to remove the junk from our lives and to build His structure in us. Of course they may not even understand that they are just contractors and their services would be terminated when the job is completed. They may be deceived into thinking that they are the landowner.

We need to be confident that we are being built to specifications and that God's guiding hands are in control over every situation and circumstance that we go through. And be assured that we will not be destroyed in the process. When we pass through troubles that have the potential to destroy us, we need to remember that

God is with us and will see us through every hardship that we face. "When you go through deep waters and great trouble, I will be with you. When you go through rivers of difficulty, you will not drown! When you walk through the fire of oppression, you will not be burned up; the flames will not consume you." Isaiah 43:2. With this promise in mind we need to stay focused, being diligent and not be dismayed in the face of hardship.

We need to train our minds to appropriately respond to changes, and our spirits to listen to the voice of the Holy Spirit and obey, since He is the one who will guide us into our place of purpose. The Holy Spirit will also teach us the secrets of humility, so that we could access that which God has in store for us.

Had Ruth not humbled herself and gone to the barley fields after she arrived in Israel she would never have been as blessed as she was. It was law and custom in Israel for harvesters not to pick up grains that would have fallen but to leave them for the poor to gather. "Blessed are the poor in spirit for theirs is the kingdom of heaven." Matthew 5:3 It is only when we humble ourselves and admit that we are poor and seek to access Gods provisions will we be able to experience the "grains" of blessings that heaven has reserved for us. It is only when we would have placed ourselves in God's need line will we be able to pick up the blessings he has left on purpose for us.

Our Greatest Tragedy

Sin is the mother of all tragedies. Everyone who would have ever walked the face of this earth was kissed by sin. Romans 3:23 tell us thus, "For all have sinned and fall short of the glory of God". Sin is worst than any cancer and it works in the hearts and lives of the people God created so that it can alluringly drag those that it would have deceptively trapped, away from God to their death and destruction.

The essence of sin is not about do's and don'ts, rather it is about the lack of a right relationship with God the Heavenly Father. Sin has hindered mankind from having that experience. Generally, we understand that a healthy relationship with those around us and with those who are important to us is invaluable. In many cases our tragedy and emotional traumas emanates from distorted, damaged, and destroyed relationships.

However, there is no tragedy greater than living without the glory of right relationship with our creator. Even though we may have overcome many tragedies before, it is only upon overcoming this tragedy that we would have truly overcome. The beautiful thing is, although sin is the greatest of all tragedies, it is the easiest to overcome. Salvation in and through Jesus Christ is the remedy for the tragedy of sin because Jesus places us in a right relationship with our Heavenly Father.

Romans 10:9-10 has this to say about Salvation "But if you acknowledge and confess with your lips that Jesus is Lord and in your heart believe (adhere to, trust in, and rely on the truth) that God raised Him from the dead, you will be saved. For with the heart a person believes (adhere to, trust in, and rely on Christ) and so is justified (declared righteous, acceptable to God), and with the mouth he confesses (declares openly and speaks out freely his faith) *and* confirms [his] salvation".

Below is a prayer of salvation for those who need to make their relationship right with God their Heavenly Father.

Prayer for Salvation

Dear God I come to you today, in the name of Jesus Christ your Son. I have come to confess , that He, Jesus is Lord, I believe with all my heart that you raised Him from the dead. O God I am asking you to forgive all of my sins, wash, cleanse and purify me in the blood of your dear Son.

Father, I am also asking that you deliver me from the tragedy of sin and redeem me from its consequences. My desire is to live daily in right relationship with you. I am asking you to teach me by the power of your Spirit how to live my life the way you would have preordained. Amen.

CHAPTER TWO

A Foreign Woman's Search for Grace

> And Ruth the Moabitess said to Naomi, Let me now go to the field, and glean ears of corn after *him* in whose sight I shall find grace. And she said unto her, Go, my daughter.   Ruth 2:2

A Foreigner

The book Ruth in the Bible is a very small one containing only four chapters. It bears the name of the young woman who so graciously stands out in it. In this book Ruth made a decision to move from her homeland to another country. Wrapped in this decision was the hard, cold reality that in this new place of abode she was no longer a native but a foreigner.

The character Ruth is a practical representation of the spiritual status of an unredeemed person. Everyone who has not come into the salvation experience or those who are not in right relationship with their Heavenly Father, is considered by God as strangers, foreigners and aliens, in other words a people who absolutely do not belong to Him. We may say to ourselves, "But God created us all, so we belong to Him." In this manner yes, God created us; His breath of life sustains us. However, this does mean that we all have a relationship with Him. It is the relationship which separates those who are His from those we are not His. Isaiah 59:2 tells us this, "But your iniquities have made a separation

19

between you and your God, and your sins have hidden His face from you so that He will not hear". Iniquity basically speaks of the habitual and the presumptuous sins people practice. God is holy, this means that He does not sin. God created the first man and woman like himself, holy. God intended that the first man and woman would reproduce and fill the earth with holy people thus; God would enjoy a loving relationship with his creation. The first man disobeyed God and so changes everything. As a result man forfeited his glory and became different from God. This made it impossible for God to have the relationship He desired to have with His creation.

The inescapable truth is this; nature would always be reflected in actions and actions are a direct representation of one's culture or lifestyle. When Adam sinned it changed his nature of holiness to a sinful one. With this change of nature in Adam came a change of relationship with God. God was still holy, Adam was now sinful. Naturally Adam still belonged to God, but relationship wise he did not, sin had severed that connection. Thus Adam was now separated from God; he had become a foreigner. Not only had he lost the nature of God but he was no longer influenced by the culture which God had created in the Garden of Eden. In fact Adam was thrown out of Eden. We were all in Adam when he sinned, as he was the first man; we all came to earth through him. Therefore, his new culture, being dominated by sin became our culture. He also lost his status as a "citizen" of God's kingdom; this loss of status also became our loss.

The book of Ruth amplifies this truth about us being foreigners without Christ. Of the four chapters in the book of Ruth we see this young woman being referred to as "Ruth the Moabitess" on four distinctive occasions.

She was for the first time singled out as the "Moabitess" which was a polite word for foreigner, after entering the country of Israel with Naomi in Ruth 1:22. In Moab she was just Ruth. There was no need to single her out by the name of her country because she was at home. Everything about her reflected her nation's culture. The language she spoke, her manner of dress, her choice of food and her personal preferences were influenced by her culture. In the same way, people on the earth are influenced and consequently governed by two opposing kingdoms and cultures. These are namely the kingdom of God and the kingdom of Satan. In the kingdom of God which is characterized by righteousness, peace and joy, Jesus is Lord. In the kingdom of Satan which is also referred to as the kingdom of darkness, Satan rules and he lords over his subjects. This kingdom is characterized by pride, deception and hate. Every nation and kingdom has laws or a structured system which governs its people; this is referred to as the constitution. In every nation and kingdom citizens and those who live there have a distinct way of living or lifestyle, which is referred to as their culture. So also is the kingdom of God. On earth, anyone who is not influenced by the culture of the constitution of the Kingdom of God, which is the Bible, is referred to as a sinner, unbeliever, non Christian by those living in accordance to the culture of the Kingdom of God. However, these individuals amongst their peers and others like themselves would not be singled out because they all have similar lifestyles. It is only as they encounter people with a different lifestyle would they become conscious of this culture difference. This is because someone is only a foreigner when he or she is outside of his or her homeland or accepted culture. When the culture of the Kingdom of God does not govern our lives, God considers us as strangers and foreigners.

The second time Ruth was singled out as the "Moabitess" was in Ruth 2:2 on the occasion in which she was making a request of Naomi her mother-in-law who was a citizen of the country of Israel. Ruth wanted to glean the field of someone who would favorably accept her. Ruth was aware that the culture in which she now lived was alien to her. She was a Moabitess in Israel. Nations offer rights, privileges and access to their citizens. Since she did not have that "citizen" status she knew that finding grace or favor in the eyes of a kind person could have turned things around for her. So she went in search of it. Standing in a garage does not make someone an automobile. In like manner attending church, giving offering, tithing and being involved in church activities do not make someone a citizen of the Kingdom of God. Activities do not attest to citizenship, culture does. By our own efforts we cannot make the shift from being foreigners to citizens. In most countries the privilege of citizenship can be granted by living in that country for a number of years or being born to a citizen of that country. In the kingdom of God the privilege of citizenship is granted only through being born again. The birth, death and resurrection of Jesus Christ made this privilege of being born again available to all.

The third occasion where Ruth was referred to as the "Moabitess" was in Ruth 2:21 when she was testifying to Naomi that she encountered a man who was exceptionally kind to her. It was God's divine providence which influenced Ruth's decision to move to Israel. God had a plan to use her life as a testimony of the grace He will lavishly bestow upon those who will search for it.

She was referred to as "Ruth the Moabitess" in Chapter 4:10 for the fourth and last time by Boaz, a next of kin to her husband Mahlon, father-in-law Elimelech and brother in law Chilion. This was the man who showed her expectional kindness. Boaz made this reference because he was reminding the elders and the people gathered at the city gate that they were witnesses to the transaction of his redeeming or buying back of all that belonged to Elimelech, Chilion and Mahlon from the hand of Naomi, including Ruth since she was Mahlon's widow.

A Time for Grace

God's grace is a voluntary expression of his loving kindness toward us. This loving kindness expresses itself in provision. God's provision sets in place the supply needed to satisfy an existing or an expected need. Ruth moved to Israel with nothing to depend on and no one to provide for her. She needed food. God divinely influenced the time she moved to Israel which was at the beginning of the barley harvest, a time when food was in supply. She understood that the barley harvest would not go on forever. This was why, in making the request to go to the barley field she said to her mother-in-law; "Let me *now* go..." Ruth 2:2.

God also knew that we would need grace because of our "foreign" spiritual status. He, therefore, placed us on the earth at a time when it is in abundant supply, Jesus being already crucified. His crucifixion has made the way for us to restore that broken relationship between God and us. We too, must understand that this period of grace would not go on forever. Today is our day of grace. 2 Corinthians 6:2 ...behold, now *is* the accepted time; behold, now *is* the day of salvation.

Because we are in this period of grace we are not immediately made to pay the penalty for sin. Instead we are granted the privilege of time in which to repent. Repentance simply means that we make a conscious decision to stop offending God and begin to please him with our thoughts and actions. We must also understand that the opportunity for repentance is a privilege granted and not an obligation due.

A Set Time of Grace for the Unsaved

There is a set time of grace for those who need to turn from their sins. Genesis 6:3 tells us this, "And the Lord said, My spirit shall not always strive with man, for that he also is flesh: yet his days shall be a hundred and twenty days." God said this against the back drop of a time like ours. A time in which people did whatever their wicked imaginations conceived. These people were exposed to His grace when He was calling them to repent from their sins through His servant Noah. They were warned of an impending judgment, but these people did not believe. We are exposed to His grace through the work of the Holy Spirit which is to convict and convince the world of sin, righteousness and judgment, as stated in John 16:8.

The Holy Spirit does this convicting and convincing through people who share the good news by various means. The good news of God's saving grace towards man is announced through personal contact, like one-on-one witnessing. It is done through evangelistic preaching at crusades in local areas, local churches and on television. The knowledge of God's saving grace could be attained through books and magazines. This message is, however, being taken for granted; some people do not believe. They are convinced that they do not need the grace which Jesus Christ offers. The spirits of this age of modernization, technology and newageism have blinded people's minds. Some people believe that this world will not end, rather we would evolve. Yet others believe that this world will end but they have some time to play with, so they postpone receiving the grace of Jesus Christ. But time is slippery, one moment we have lots of it and the next we are completely out of time. Folks back in Noah's days were allotted years to live in handsome three figures. Their days were much longer, but eventually it expired and their judgment was upon them. A great flood came and they were all destroyed. Now we know that people in our time do not live to be one hundred and twenty years. In fact if someone manages to live to be one hundred years he or she would be elated, and the achievement very much celebrated by others. We must not ignore the fact that our days are much shorter. It is also noteworthy that the Holy Spirit will not convict sinners all their lives of their sins. There will be a period or periods when the opportunities for individual repentance will be orchestrated. After constant refusal to change the Holy Spirit will leave that person alone.

A Time of Grace for the Saved

There is a set time of grace for Christians who struggle with sin. The word struggle implies a great effort, or a fight, to resist. Struggling with sin does not mean that the battle is lost, but that the fight is still very much on. Christians struggle with sin because they were born with a sinful nature. Before they became Christians they lived according to this nature. Becoming a Christian or the salvation experience does not mean that an individual will immediately quit committing all the sins he or she practiced before this experience and begin to act holy. While some sinful habits are immediately dropped others are dropped with time as these individuals become matured in the nature of Christ, which is holiness. Some habits go through prayer and sometimes fasting, others with counseling and deliverance.

When we come to Christ we must aggressively deal with those sins which dominated us in the past, as these are the ones which will become our source of defeat, should we be neglectful. Aggressively dealing with sinful habits means taking the necessary steps to ensure that we stifle the old nature to death. It may mean that we avoid further association with some people, some places and avoid inappropriate conversations. It will certainly mean doing what the Apostle Paul did. In 1 Corinthians 15:31 He said, "...I die daily [face death every day and die to self]." Dying daily is what we should all do to our lustful desires, thus killing the old nature of sin.

Dying daily is a deliberate and sometimes a painful act. There are some sinful habits that we struggle to give up because of the pleasure it brought in times past, because of character weakness, or prevailing circumstances. Whatever our reason for struggling with sin the devil has a way of down playing sin by making us think that it is not that bad or that every believer is living in some sort of sin. This lie clouds out the truth that God has given us everything pertaining to life and godliness. Since God has totally equipped us for victory then we have no excuse to live defeated lives. This is why there is a set time of grace for Christians who struggle with sin. A thought provoking question was and is still being asked in Romans 6:1. "What shall we say then? Shall we continue in sin, that grace may abound? Verse 2 says, "God forbid. How shall we, that are dead to sin, live any longer therein?"

Fields of Grace

Before grace was made accessible to us, man lived in accordance to the law that was given by God to Moses. There were basically three types of laws. Firstly, there was the ceremonial law; this specifically related to worship. Secondly, there was the civil law which applied to daily living, and thirdly, there was the moral law, of which the Ten Commandments are an example.

It was law in Israel that during the harvesting of crops that the corners of fields not be harvested and the grains which had fallen during harvesting were not to be picked-up. These were to be left for the poor and foreigners to gather, Leviticus 19: 9-10.

God made provision for two sets of people; the poor and the foreigner.

I consider it significant that the first of the beatitudes in Matthew chapter five addresses the poor by calling them blessed. It says, "Blessed are the poor in spirit for theirs is the kingdom of heaven". Poor in spirit is not synonymous with material impoverishment. Being poor in spirit imply a lowliness of the attitude of one's heart. The woman who is poor in spirit is the woman who would have come to a place of humility. She would have recognized that above all she needs God. He has everything she needs and she is nothing without Him. She would have recognized that she needs others. A woman who is poor in spirit would have grown into the understanding that she is better than no one and as such would have learnt to esteem others higher than herself. Having such an attitude will enable every woman to access and sustain that which God has in store for her.

Ruth was able to go into the fields to pick up leftovers because she acted in accordance with the law concerning harvesting. Firstly she was a foreigner, secondly she was poor. This woman was not in delusion of who she was, she did not pretend to have what she did not and she allowed nothing and no one to stand in her way. Too many of us allow pride and pretence to stand between us and our place of grace.

To her these grains of barley meant a supply of food, as grains speak of provision. To us a supply may not necessarily mean food, but it may be the strength to go on, peace of mind, courage, a job, a house, a car or that which God alone has the ability to supply. Whatever that need is God possess the capacity to satisfy. When we acknowledge that God alone can satisfy all of our needs and lean on his kindness, we are steps closer to having our needs met. A field speaks of continuity; when a person has a field, be it through ownership or access he or she is sure of provision for the future. To Ruth accessing grain meant that her personal needs and that of the older woman she cared for would be satisfied. Their provider was taken away; this forced her to become a provider for herself and Naomi. However, Ruth did not want grain from just any field. She wanted to gather where she was favoured. Many women find themselves in this place where they become the provider in their households because of many reasons. These women are required to provide not only for the physical but emotional, social and spiritual needs of their household. A task which could be quite wearying, overwhelming and sometimes seemingly unrewarding. Beneath the burden of this load a woman can be broken.

As you reorganize your life after hard experiences you should be mindful in which field you enter. Hard experiences make you vulnerable and fragile. When you are like this you are not always thoughtful. It is at this point in your life that you must always remember to act wisely. Be careful of whom you trust and confide in. You must resist the desire to pour out your heart to everyone who will listen. Not because someone listens to you means that he or she cares for you or is trustworthy. Trust should grow as a friendship grows. It is always better to deal with people whom you just met on a need to know basis, regardless of how warm they may seem. You should not tell people more than they need to know. Do not answer questions which were not asked; do not feel obligated to give answers for every question asked. As a test of genuineness, give those who come into your life a little bit of your story at a time. See how they handle the little you entrusted them with; from this you would know if you can go on to trusting.

I was told about the plight of a single mother who was too trusting. I will refer to her as Jenny for the purposes of this book. She was and still is a Christian. Jenny was gainfully employed but still found it difficult to pay all of her bills and take care of herself and her young child. From time to time caring relatives assisted financially. Over time Jenny developed a close relationship with her supervisor who was also a female and a Christian. Her supervisor seems to love God very much as she constantly talked about his word, and about praying, fasting, about listening to gospel messages at home. This supervisor projected the overall image of being a committed believer and a kind caring human being. Jenny concluded that since her supervisor was a God fearing person she could be trusted. So she let this woman into the secret place of her emotional, social and financial struggles. In fact they both shared their struggles with one another. But Jenny's new confidant was not as loyal to her as she thought. This woman told Jenny's secrets to her other friends. She mocked and laughed at Jenny behind her back but talked about God in her presence. People began to warn Jenny about her new friend. They also told her about her friend's disloyalty but Jenny did not believe. She was convinced that she had truly encountered a God fearing woman. However, Jenny finally recognized the evil in her friend when God placed a man in her life who loves her. She got married and life began to change for her. Her friend began to openly act devilish and said even more evil things. When confronted, Jenny's friend confessed that she was jealous of the good things which are happening to Jenny. Jenny related that she was hurt and disappointed and could have reacted by letting her friend's secrets out but she decided to treat this experience as an opportunity to become a wiser person.

It is also noteworthy that not because someone can relate to your experience means that God will use that person to help you. Some will use your situation to exploit and control you. Therefore, resist the temptation to be "needy", acting wisely, working diligently with your hands and trusting God to supply your needs will close the door of being exploited. Being sensitive to the Holy Spirit will save you additional heartache for He will lead you to the right people. Ruth was young but wise; she understood that grace or favour in the eyes of the right person would make a difficult situation light and manageable. Like her, we must seek grace. God is full of grace towards us. When we ask, he will give it to us. We must pray that God grants us favour with himself and with people.

When God's grace is upon us it will release many blessings and draw great favour towards us. We must remember that whatever grace has brought to us grace must keep for us, be it a successful business, economic prosperity, a strong marriage, good kids, healthy friendships or spiritual gifts. There will be times when we will be tempted to think our achievements are our self effort or, our family background, our good deeds and that we deserve what we have. None of us deserve anything. Thus, a humble attitude is important. There may be some practical things that we may have to do in order to maintain a humble spirit. The fight to remain humble may be intense but the fight is winning. Continuously walking in humility will cause us to come into a more intimate relationship with Christ. This walk must be expressed in total dependence on Him. We indicate this dependence by spending more time in prayer, waiting in His presence, through fasting, in worship, by renewing our minds in the Word of God. It is as we depend on Him that we decrease in ourselves and He increases in us. When Christ increases in us His will and desires become our will and desires, and ultimately there is a unity of hearts, that of the creator and the created.

As we set out to seek we will be confronted with the choice of should be sought first, be it a field, grain or grace; exceptional kindness from God. What we seek first we will find first and what we find will determine the acuteness of the change we experience.

Finding a field first, will give the hope that we will continue to live, but a field also means hard work and little rest. Finding grain first will result in the present need being sustained for a short time. Finding grain first will mean a continuous search, or chasing after things which sometimes elude us. Finding grace first will satisfy not only our present needs but we will be assured of continued provision. Ruth went in search of grace and she found it. This is what Boaz said to her, "...Listen my daughter, do not go to glean in another field or leave this one, but stay here close to my maidens. Watch which field they reap, and follow them. Have I not charged the young men not to molest you? And when you are thirsty, go to the vessels and drink what the young men have drawn," Ruth 2:8,9.

Grace constantly gives. Grace only adds and never takes nor come empty handed. Grace will cause us to become creative in meaningful ways, cause us to be shown unusual kindness from those whom we least expected. Grace will cause limitations and inabilities to be lifted from our lives. Grace will introduce us to the right people. It will give us what we never had so that we can go where we have never gone. Grace enables us to create tangible realities for those whose lives we were destined to touch in spite of what we have been through. Grace is God's unmerited favor and His divine ability. We will only be able to access what we seek when we seek grace, we will find it if we seek for it with our whole heart. In Matthew 6:33, Jesus counsels us in this direction. "But seek (aim at and strive after) first of all His kingdom and His righteousness (His way of doing and being right), and *then* all these things taken together will be given you besides."

Drink your Fill of the Lord

In Ruth 2:9 Boaz said to Ruth "And when you are thirsty, go to the vessels and drink..." Every physical need has a parallel spiritual need. Natural water is refreshing and thirst quenching to our bodies. Water also represents the life giving power of the Holy Spirit. In our souls, we thirst for the refreshing power of the Holy Spirit. It is significant that when Boaz made water available to Ruth, he did so without restraint. She was free to have as much as she needed. Christ made the water of life available to us through His death on the cross and by sending us the Holy Spirit. In His conversation with the woman at the well Jesus made this statement, "Jesus said to her, If you had only known *and* had recognized God's gift and Who this is that is saying to you, Give me a drink, you would have asked Him [instead] and He would have given you living water", John 4:10. In John 10:10 He further complements this statement. "...I came that they may have and enjoy life, and have it in abundance (to the full till it overflows)". There is no limit to abundance. This abundant life that Christ made available is for both now and eternity.

Enjoying abundant life now means living free of the life destroying powers of fear. This includes each and every kind of fear; the fear of rejection and failure, the fear of death and destruction, fear of disappointment, fear of having a broken marriage and of having wayward children, the fear of dying from hereditary sicknesses, the fear of poverty and lack and the fear of fear itself. Fear will stifle life out of us. God has not given us a spirit of fear, 2 Timothy 1:7. 1 John 4:18 tells us this, "There is no fear in love [dread does not exist], but full-grown (complete, perfect) love turns fear out of doors *and* expels every trace of terror! Fear brings with it the thought of punishment, and [so] he who is afraid has not reached the full maturity of love [is not yet grown into love's complete perfection]". Christ loves us perfectly; this means that there are no reservations about his loving us. And we are not expected to meet any requirements in order to win His love. He loves us because He chose to love us. Loving and being loved adds meaning and fullness to our lives. Understanding that we are simply, purely and lavishly loved by God will result in the living of our lives to the fullest.

Experts say that water hydrates the body. While doing this it acts as a natural moisturizer for the skin making it fresh, flush and youthful. However, this only happens as correct measures are taken daily. The same thing will happen to our spirit when we daily drink of the Lord. When we drink of the Lord we allow the Holy Spirit to pour out his ability, wisdom, strength and knowledge into us. It is while drinking that new and fresh revelation will flow to us. This is the place where creative ideas for business, personal advancement and the power to earn money are released. It is also while drinking that we come into new methods of dealing with situations and people. When the Word of God becomes as necessary and as satisfying as drinking a glass of water we will begin to experience peace which is beyond human understanding, unshakable confidence and great strength. Resulting in a renewed and refreshed life despite what we are going through more so as we continue to hold fast to the refreshing truth of the Word of God.

Measures of Grace

There are measures of grace. The measure each person walk in is influenced by God's purpose for his life and according to the level that he can contain. We enlarge our capacity for a greater measure of grace through humility. When Boaz showed kindness to Ruth by telling her to continue to glean in his field and to drink from his vessels the scripture tells that she bowed herself to the ground, and said to him, "Why have I found grace in your eyes, that you should notice me, when I am a foreigner?"Ruth 2:10. Ruth bowed in humble acknowledgement and appreciation to the one who has been gracious to her. The lack of humility is a stumbling block for many believers. From the moment they gain any recognition for being gifted or talented in any way they adapt a larger than life attitude. There is a woman I know, she loved God and was passionate about doing his will. As she submitted herself to the Lord, His anointing and grace rested upon her life in a tremendous way. God began to use her to do great things. Many people came to received healing and help from God. However, pride began to creep in when she was caught up with the applause of the people. Her relationship with the Lord was gradually replaced with popularity and she began to treat the people who followed her as fans. She worked hard to keep them fascinated and happy. They became the main source of influence in her life and affected how she prayed, what she preached and prophesied. This woman began to minister in favour of her friends and associates and against those who were not. God in his mercy sent someone to warn her. But rather than seize this opportunity to repent she ignored it and continued in her ways. Today this woman is not where she was in the Lord. She cultivated an arrogant attitude and it shifted her out of place.

We must acknowledge the reality that we live in a society in which we are constantly bombarded with visual flaunting of success stories, attractive imagery of fame and fortune, and endless displays of the glamour and glory of the lifestyles of stars, superstars and wannabe stars. This has without doubt, created in our minds the temptation to be vain glorious. Therefore, some believers have come to view the church as a place for stardom. This is one of the reasons why there is so much fighting and competition in the church. We have completely forgotten that we are in this world but we are not of it! And the way up in man's eyes is the way down in God's sight. Jesus told us concerning these things, "Not so shall it be among you; but whoever wishes to be great among you *must* be your servant, Matthew 20:26 (emphasis added). Therefore the call to ministry and the recognition as an anointed son of God is the call not to stardom but to servanthood! Thus, after we would have recognized that there is a calling and specific gifts of the Holy Spirit operate in us, straight away it should be understood that we have been granted a unique opportunity. Therefore, it is time for us to get off our high chairs, roll up our sanctified sleeves and get down to where the people of God are and begin to serve them.

A Place of Communion

Ruth was able to walk in a greater level of grace simply because she knew how to humble herself. "At mealtime Boaz said to her, come here and eat of the bread and dip your morsel in the sour wine," Ruth 2:14. She was invited to a place of communion. The place of communion is not a place for the common person. It is a place reserved for people who are in close relationship with each other. It is significant that before Jesus was crucified he sat to have communion with those who were closest to Him, His disciples. At this communion they were given a meal of bread which represented His body and wine which represented His blood which was to be shed. They were told to take this communal meal as often as possible in remembrance of Christ, Luke 22:17-19. Ruth sat in this place of communion with Boaz as a foretaste for those of us who will partake in the communion of Christ's body and blood. Throughout this book Boaz is presented as a typology or representation of Jesus Christ. This will be made even clearer in future chapters.

Few believers ever enter into a communal relationship with Christ. I am not talking about eating bread and drinking wine. Many believers go to their local churches and partake of the bread and wine ceremoniously and walk away without understanding the significance of their actions thus are deprived of the power associated with it.

The place of communion is a place of common union. It is the place where we become one with Christ and one with each other. We become one with Christ when we acknowledge and respond positively to the truth that His body was broken and His blood was shed for us on the cross of Calvary. We become one with each other because of the common belief and acceptance of this truth. We bring this truth to our remembrance when we partake of communion in our local churches by eating of the same loaf of bread and drinking of the same wine. When we do this we are saying to each other, your struggles are my struggles, your fights are my fights, your enemy is my enemy, your strengths are my strengths and your victories are my victories because we are one. We are members of the same body, which is Christ's. But, it is sad to acknowledge, that we have moved away from this understanding and although we stand together at the altar and partake of the same sacramental items we walk back to our seats separated, void of the understanding of our actions and robbed of the power and strength which comes through unity.

When we partake of the communal sacraments we partake of Christ, thus we have access to his strength in our weaknesses, and to his ability in our limitations, we are able to access the God kind of faith so that doubt fades into a distant shadow of the past and our fears are replaced with confidence and hope.

When we are in true communion with Christ we understand that this is a level of relationship in which Christ sees us as His bretheren and we understand that God His father is our heavenly father and we are all sons of God. "But as many as received him, to them gave he power to become the sons of God, *even* to them that believe on his name: Which were born, not of blood, nor of the will of the flesh, nor of the will of man, but of God", John 1:12,13.

This level of relationship not only gives us access to everything He possesses but also seats us where He is seated. "And raised us up together, *and made us sit together in the heavenly places in Christ Jesus*", Ephesians 2:6, (emphasis added).

A Place of Recognition

The place of communion is a place where we are able to recognize each other because we are seated together in Christ. This is not a physical place but a spiritual one. Therefore, a son of God should be able to recognize another son even though in the natural they may not be acquainted with one another. This brings to light the fact that in reality this is not so because of our attitude towards one another.

We readily become suspicious of each other; we build personality profile of each other by way of hearsay and gossip. This inability to recognize each other as sons of the same heavenly father creates occasion for lying, hate, jealously, envy and bitterness amongst brethren. This should not be so. We need to allow the spirit of God to bring us in alignment with each other.

Build Relationships

My thought provoking question is this, "Can we know the Lord Jesus Christ by simply listening to who people say He is? The answer is no. Absolutely not! We can only claim to know the Lord by having a relationship with Him, even in the boundaries of this relationship it would still be unsafe to act as though we know all about him. Similarly, how is it that even before knowing each other properly, building proper friendship, or spending quality time with each other, we run around claiming to know each other and pompously making inflammatory statements about each other? Whilst this is easy to do, seeking to build good relationships is more beneficial.

There are times that we may need to have quality knowledge about the person we allow in our lives or in leadership in our local church. However, the sources from which we solicit information reveals a lot about us and the level of relationship we have with the Lord. Sons of God, firstly, ask their Heavenly father and rely on the Holy Spirit to reveal the trustworthiness of the brethren. Secondly, people with godly integrity turn to people with godly integrity to advise in this regard.

Boaz

Who was this man Boaz? He was a descendant of Rahab. A near relative of Naomi's husband, Elimelech. A farmer by occupation and an honourable, wealthy businessman who lived in Bethlehem. His relationship to Naomi's husband meant that he could be a kinsman –redeemer. A kinsman-redeemer is a close male relative who could be approached for rescue in times of difficulties. "And her mother-in-law said to her, "Where have you gleaned today? Where did you work? Blessed be the man who noticed you. So [Ruth] told [her], The name of him with whom I worked today is Boaz. And Naomi said to her daughter-in-law , Blessed be he of the Lord who has not ceased his kindness to the living and the dead. And she said to her, the man is a near relative of ours, one who has the right to redeem us", Ruth 2:19-20.

In this book of typology and representations, this man Boaz is a representation or a typology of Christ. He possesses honor, power, riches and all that is necessary to redeem a next of kin. The title "next of kin" is used in relation to a person's closest blood relative.

A kinsman possesses the right to redeem and restore his relative. Once approached, he could do this in several ways. Firstly, he could redeem his relative if that relative is obligated to sell himself as a slave to someone to clear his indebtedness to that person or merely because he is poor. Thus, a kinsman could redeem and restore to him his freedom. The kinsman also had the right to buy back any inheritance his relative would have forfeited. Secondly, the kinsman possessed the right to seek vengeance on behalf of his relative if that relative was murdered. Thus, the relative's blood would have been avenged when the kinsman killed his relative murderer. Thirdly, the levirate law in Deuteronomy 25:5-10, indicates that when a brother died without a child his widow should not marry outside the family, instead she should marry her husband's brother. This would enable him to raise an heir for his dead brother and as such continue his brother's name and inheritance. If there were no brothers then the closest blood relative could be approached to play this role. As unusual as it sounds there was a reason for this. The best way for a person to be remembered was through his descendents, if the childless widow marries outside the family it would bring to an end the lineage of her first husband. In this case Naomi had no more sons. Therefore, it was necessary that she look to a near relative to perform the duty of a kinsman-redeemer. In addition to raising an heir, the redeemer also redeemed or bought back any family property that was sold, and repaid any outstanding debts. If a widow desired to be redeemed she was usually the one to take the initiative in approaching the redeemer.

Boaz's role as kinsman to Naomi granted him the right to redeem the inheritance of Elimelech and to take Ruth as wife. However, there was a kinsman who was nearer to Naomi than Boaz. Although Boaz was asked by Ruth to take the responsibility as redeemer, the nearer kinsman possessed the rights over Boaz. Being an honorable man, Boaz not only informed Ruth about the existence of this nearer kinsman but he approached this kinsman on Ruth's behalf.

"Then Boaz went up to the city's gate and sat down there, and behold, the kinsman of whom Boaz had spoken came by. He said to him, Ho! Turn aside and sit down here. So he turned aside and sat down. And Boaz took ten men of the elders of the city and said, Sit down here. And they sat down. And he said to the kinsman, Naomi, who had returned from the country of Moab, had sold the parcel of land which belonged to our brother Elimelech. And I thought to let you hear of it, saying. Buy it in the presence of those sitting here and before the elders of my people. If you will redeem it, redeem it; but if you will not redeem it, then say so, that I may know; for there is no one besides you to redeem it, and I am [next of kin] after you. And he said, I will redeem it. Boaz said, The day you buy the field of Naomi, you must buy also Ruth the Moabitess, the widow of the dead man. To restore the name of the dead to his inheritance. And the kinsman said, I cannot redeem it for myself, least [by marrying a Moabitess] I endanger my own inheritance. Take my right of redemption yourself, for I cannot redeem it. Ruth 4:1-6

Our Boaz

"And the Redeemer shall come to Zion, and unto them that turn from transgression in Jacob, saith the Lord", Isaiah 59:20. The punctuations of genealogies which are listed throughout the Bible are quite obvious, they are more than just the listing of names. But most of us find them uninteresting so we either skip or skim through them. However, genealogy was important to the Jews since they wanted to be able to prove that they are descendents of Abraham thus heir to the promised blessings. Its recordings support for us that the One sent into this world to redeem it was indeed a descendant of Abraham. Now we know that we who believe are sons of Abraham because of our faith. In the Gospel of Luke 3:23-38 as we read the account of Jesus' genealogy we see Luke going way back to Adam, this shows us that Jesus Christ, the promised Messiah, is related to us all. This is why we see it stated of him in Hebrews 2:12 saying "I will declare your name to my brethren..." The name Jesus means Saviour. When the angel of the Lord visited Joseph in a dream he told him that the child in Mary's womb was conceived by the Holy Spirit and He should be called Jesus because He will save his people from their sins, Matthew 1:20, 21. The name Christ is not Jesus' surname but a title which has the same meaning as the word Messiah. Messiah means anointed one. Jesus is called Christ because he is the one God chose and sent to earth as Saviour. When Jesus came to earth he was totally man; born of a virgin. He looked like any other human baby. He was also totally God who came to us as Emmanuel. God came to earth taking the form of man with flesh and blood so that he could redeem lost mankind back to Himself. Mary's boy child, Jesus Christ is our nearest kinsman and the one who has the right to redeem us. He is our Boaz!

As stated earlier, widowed women and persons sold into slavery because of poverty, debt or a criminal offence could have been redeemed by a kinsman who possessed the capacity and willingness to pay the price for the freedom of his relative. The price paid for the freedom of a slave was referred to as a ransom. The person being bought back is called the redeemed and the kinsman doing the act of buying back is called the redeemer. "If a man sells his daughter as a servant, she is not to go free as menservants do. If she does not please the master who has selected her for himself, he must let her be redeemed. He has no right to sell her to foreigners, because he has broken faith with her. If he selects her for his son, he must grant her the rights of a daughter". Exodus 21:7-9 Adam the first man became a slave to sin when he disobeyed God's instruction. Thus, he sold us all into slavery of sin.

In our modern world of great explosion of freedom and liberty there are fathers who still sell their daughters into a life of physical slavery. This happens in some countries on the African continent and in places in the Middle East and Asia. There are fathers who sold their daughters as slaves to a life of sin because they did not fulfill their mandated roles as father, provider, protector and one who rules over his house well. There are fathers who broke faith with their daughters by rejecting them as their own, thus subjecting their lives to abuse. Our heavenly father desires that every daughter be redeemed; he had already paid the price for her ransom even before she was born.

"Then I passed by and saw you kicking about in your blood, and as you lay there in your blood I said to you, Live!" Ezekiel 16:6. We were all born as helpless sinners destined to receive the wages of death at the end of our lives. Imbedded in our nature is the desire to live. People instinctively resist death. We aggressively fight against the very thought of death and would spend our life's savings trying to stay alive should a life threatening situation arise. Billions of dollars and years of research are spent to make better drugs and to find cures which will combat terminal diseases. People will deny their cravings of pleasant tasting food for ones that, reportedly, will make them live longer. They will stick to rigid routine of diet and exercises that promise longevity. The average woman spends more than half of her life working to earn so that she may live.

Most religion teaches about life after death; be it through reincarnation or living in another place after leaving this world. For what it's worth we all want to live. The devil had stolen life from us; not only eternal life but our ability to live a full and satisfying life here on earth. God saw us in our helpless state unable to recover from the lost of our relationship with him. Furthermore, He knows that we cannot experience the fullness that we desire by our own efforts and so has come to our aid. Christ came to give us life and life in all of its fullness. When he came he relieved us from striving by offering us His life as a free gift, fully and eternally by his death.

Sicknesses and diseases are excluded from the renewed life in Christ. Therefore, illnesses will certainly be trespassing, touching our lives. Of course we may not live in a perpetual state of happiness but we are sure to find satisfaction, peace and joy. And when we die physically we can rest assured that we will be resurrected to live forever with Him in his second coming to this earth. Therefore, we can now approach the issues of life with the knowledge of our freedom in Christ knowing that Christ has already paid the price to buy us back, and we are now free from the chains of slavery to sin and its consequences.

The Price of Redemption

Every child born into this world was born to live for a purpose but Mary's boy child Jesus Christ was born to die for a purpose. Why was his death necessary? Because, the wages of sin is death and sin has a committed paymaster. At the appointed time sin would have gladly given us our dues. To be severed from the ties of this obligation we needed someone who would willingly trade places with us. Hebrew 9:22 says " ...and without the shedding of blood there is neither release from sin *and* its guilt *nor* the remission of sins due *and* merited punishment for sins". This was why Israel was commanded to offer the blood of bulls and rams as a sacrifice to atone for their sins. The life of an animal had to be given in the place of a human life. These sacrifices, however, were only a temporary measure as such could not have effectively dealt with the sin issue. And these sacrifices had to be done perpetually for they could have only atone; meaning "to cover" sin rather than completely remove it. At the appointed time Christ came to earth to pay the price for our redemption.

A redeemer could have bought back a next of kin only if he had the purchasing power or the means of paying the price for their freedom. "You must know (recognize) that you were redeemed (ransomed) from the useless (fruitless) way of living inherited by tradition from [your] forefathers, not with corruptible things [such as] silver and gold, but [you were purchased] with the precious blood of Christ (the Messiah), like that of a [sacrificial] lamb without blemish or spot", 1 Peter 1:18 , 19. Blood is the price for the redemption of lost humanity; blood had to be shed because blood represents life.

Blood also determines paternity. Science proves that a child has the same blood as his father and inside the womb it is not possible for the mother's blood to become mixed with that of the unborn. Jesus blood was acceptable because it was pure as there was no trace of sin in Him. He was not born of man's will and action but of God's divine plan and power having no human parental blood in him.

CHAPTER THREE

Time for Change

Then Naomi her mother-in-law said to Ruth, My daughter, shall I not seek rest or a home for you, that you may prosper? And now is not Boaz, with whose maidens you were our relative? See, he is winnowing barley tonight at the threshing floor. Wash and anoint yourself therefore, and put on your best clothes and go down to the threshing floor...   Ruth 3:1-3

There is indeed a time for everything. As the time for one thing comes to an end the beginning of another unfolds. We call this process change. The sound of this word may induce distress on some people whilst to others the very thought of change can be that spark which rekindles their flame of hope and be the rainbow that adds fresh colour to their dreams which had faded to black and white.

Change is inevitable as we grow in our walk with Christ. The Bible tells us about being changed from glory to glory. And God promised to make all things work together for the good of those who love Him and are called according to His purpose. Those of us who pray for change particularly in difficulties need to be reminded to be expectant as we pray. And in the midst of our expectancy we need to be conscious of the fact that answers to prayers may come in the manner we least expect. For this reason it is helpful to have those persons in our lives that can discern our season of change and so counsel us that we may advance from one level to another. The wisdom needed to advance, is always less painful and less time taking when learn through mentorship than from mistakes. Naomi knew that the time had come for change in Ruth's life, so she counselled and advised her accordingly.

Naomi advised Ruth to get cleaned up and all dressed up and go down to the threshing floor the night when Boaz was winnowing barley. As strange as Naomi's counsel may have seemed Ruth did not question nor criticize but did all that she was told. These two women had already built a relationship based on love and commitment which resulted in the trustful response of Ruth. Much more important is that, the Holy Spirit is the counsellor to every one of us who has been born again. He knows when our moment of change has come, as a matter of fact He is the one who orchestrates it. At the right time He will tell us what to do. It may involve doing things that we consider strange but because of our relationship we know that we can trust him. We must obey.

The Good Shepherd

Listening is an integral part of the change process. Before we act, we must listen. We must listen so that we may recognize who is speaking and hear what is being said to us. It is like a sheep's relationship with the shepherd. Jesus gave an illustration of Himself as the Shepherd and He said that His sheep will follow Him because they know His voice. "When he has brought his own sheep outside, he walks on before them, and the sheep follow him because they know his voice. They will never [on any account] follow a stranger, but will run away from him because they do not know the voice of strangers or recognize their call", John 10:4- 5.

Jesus, our Good Shepherd is no longer here on earth. However, He has given the gift of shepherding to many Christian leaders. These individuals who possess this gift of shepherding are spiritual leaders that we have come to know as elders and bishops but more popularly as pastors. Jesus has released in these leaders His love for the sheep, His ability to lead the sheep in the right pasture and His grace to feed and nourish the sheep. These shepherds are not owners of the sheep. They are servants of Jesus Christ, the Good Shepherd who is in heaven. The Good Shepherd, speaks through his servants. Therefore the sheep must listen to and obey the shepherds whom Christ would have placed over their lives. This does not mean that the Lord will speak only through Pastors and other spiritual Leaders. God is free to speak to us through whoever he chooses. He may choose to speak to us through a child, a co-worker, a mother, a father, a stranger. The secret is to be able to recognize when he is speaking.

Where is the Speaker Dwelling?

Talk is cheap and everyone is talking. As a person speak it is possible to discern who he or she is and where they are located spiritually. As a child, I had a little strategy I used whenever I played a game "hide and seek" with my friends and had difficulties in finding their hiding places. I used every method conceivable to get them to talk. I knew that the sound of their voices would give their locations away. This very technique can be effective spiritually. The content of believer's conversations serves as a great indicator for it reveals their level of maturity in the Lord. If we put aside all of the external stuff; portfolio and title, all that we would have heard about them and all that we think of them, then from their own lips we can know what manner of lifestyle they lead. Sometimes we may need to wait a bit and give time the opportunity to blow away the façade before we encounter the real person.

Therefore it is important that we understand that having someone in our life that can hear God for us does not negate us of the responsibility of learning to know His voice for ourselves. Every proper relationship is built on a one-to-one contract and communication. This is the same with the Lord. God always prefers to speak to us directly about our lives and issues concerning us, rather than through someone else.

Whilst listening to learn the voice of the Lord for ourselves He will point us to a place of rest even before unrest sets in. A few years ago the Lord showed me a vision concerning myself. I was at a starting line about to run a race. I was the only person in the race. I was fully clad in running gears and was doing warm up exercises. When I had finished the exercises I position myself on the starting line to listen for the sound indicating I can take off. However just before the sound went off, two hands holding a large whickered basket filled with circular paper -like material cut in diameter of about three quarter of an inch, brightly shaded with various colours on one side and adhesive on the other. The two hands holding the basket turned the entire basket over my head with the intention of completely covering me with the contents, thus I would not be able to run my race. But as this material began to fall, for the first time I noticed that I was saturated with oil and as this material fell over me they immediately slid off, not one was able to stick, but because so much adhesive came into contact with the oil on my skin I began to feel really itchy and began to scratch vigorously.

Time elapsed and I forgot what the Lord had showed me. Then the enemy released a spirit of slander against me and for a long time I was constantly bombarded with some form of character defiling gossip. I tried my best to avoid activities which created the opportunity for this, but this attempt at evasion itself created the occasion for slander. Almost everyone around me was taken by this spirit. I could not make any sense of it. Some people, whom I perceived as people who should have known better, attempted to further complicate my situation by making it their tasks to constantly attempt to bag and tag me with ungodly titles they conjured up. One day I approached a woman whom I had known for some time and who I perceived to be spiritually mature. She was aware of what was happening. I asked her what she thought could have been the possible reason for these events. Her response was, "Well, when our ways are pleasing to the Lord he will cause our enemies to be at peace with us". I was flabbergasted! Rather than giving me some words of comfort and strength this woman was implying that my ways were not pleasing to God! However I did give this woman's words some thought and I went to the Lord and asked him to show me anything in my life which was not pleasing to Him. I repented of sins I committed knowing and unknowingly yet I experienced no change.

I did get irritated and I did begin to fret. In my heart I wondered why God had not defended me? Why did he allow me to suffer in such a manner? Why did he not say something? Why did he not do something? It was as though heaven was shut up over me. When God finally broke the silence he did not say what I wanted to hear. He spoke to me about dying. John 12:24, "I tell you the truth, unless a kernel of wheat falls to the ground and die, it remains only a seed. But if it dies, it produces many seeds." At this point I concluded that if God wants me to die then it would be wiser if I surrendered to the process. I realized that there are some things we will have to go through if we are going to become who God has purposed for us to be. The process of dying to self is a hard, painful, and lonely one, because so many times people do not understand and are unable to relate to what we are going through. But when we understand where God is taking us this understanding relieves us from being caught-up in the restraints which come from being wrapped up in the need for self preservation and it frees us from the bondages which come from seeing ourselves in the reflections of the opinion of others.

Then one day the Lord reminded me of what He had showed me, and He began to counsel and advise me. He revealed to me the secret plots and the wicked intentions of some people's hearts to keep me from fulfilling my destiny. He showed me why Satan aka Slanderer was able to use the people he used to gossip and slander about me. He began to tell me what to do and what not to do, where to go and where not to go, when to go to some places and when not to go. We need to understand that God is no respecter of persons. He will expose secrets and evil intentions of everyone regardless who they are as long as they are the ones who plot mischief. What I was experiencing did not stop immediately, but I had stopped irritable and fretful because I had come to understand the necessity of being processed to fulfill purpose. I am now able to discern the heart of God in situations and I am now more acquainted with the voice of my Good Shepherd.

That experience has caused me to grow in confidence towards God, now my ears are keener to the voice of the Lord and my heart more responsive. Some unpleasant experiences our good shepherd will prevent us from encountering, others He will allow because he wants us to become more acquainted with His voice as he shepherds us through it.

Throughout our lives we may have heard many voices. We would have heard the voices of our parents', our spouse's, our relatives, our friends and associates, our spiritual leaders; we would have even heard the voice of our enemy. Listening to the clamor of many voices would have affected us in many ways. Some voices would have lead us into green pastures and some voices would have driven us into places so strange that we became frustrated and felt insecure. In a world where everyone has an opinion about and for us it is easy to become confused and loose our way if we do not know whom to listen to. In the midst of all of these voices we must incline our ears to listen continually to the voice of the Lord Jesus Christ, our Good Shepherd. His voice will heal and protect us, it will fill us with quiet confidence. We should never negate our responsibility of learning to hear His voice for ourselves.

While referring to himself as the Shepherd and stating that His sheep know His voice, we also need to note that Jesus said my sheep He did not say my lamb. This indicates a person who would have grown to maturity and is able to recognize His voice, having no doubt that the Lord has spoken without the need for a sign or further confirmation. However, the lambs could become confused and follow a stranger's voice. Sometimes lambs will miss God. Lambs can become lost or are even stolen if not guided. They need reassurance and confirmation even like little Samuel in the book of 1 Samuel when the Lord called him he thought it was Eli, the prophet. He could not have distinguished the voice of God from that of a man, but when he had grown he had no need to be coached because he had come to know the voice of God and was even able to speak and act on His behalf. Many of us may have missed God's voice in the past. Perhaps we may have thought that it was our thoughts and imaginations, or maybe it was man talking to us. Perhaps we may have known that it was God speaking to us yet we did not respond. But God will never give up on us; he will leave the ninety-nine in order to find that one lost sheep. The more we listen for His voice the clearer it will be in our hearts.

Preparation for Change - Wash

Whilst preparing Ruth to meet with Boaz, Naomi told Ruth to wash herself before she went down to the threshing floor that night. I do not think that Ruth had issues with bathing. Naomi however, told her this for emphasis. She was preparing this young woman for a date with destiny. She was seeking a home for Ruth.

She wanted her to get married and find rest in the home of her husband. Hence, Ruth was required to take extra care while preparing for this encounter.

Anytime we come into contact with destiny our lives will change. Consequently, in preparation we need to be more deliberate in what we do before this encounter. When we wash or bathe in the natural we remove the things from our outer man which had made us dirty and had given an odour. In washing there are two major requirements water and a purifying agent. Even so in the spirit we need to wash ourselves so that we will be clean and pure. One of the symbols of the Holy Spirit is water; the Holy Spirit is God on the earth, He is presently in the process of preparing us, the bride of Christ, for our encounter with Him. This is why he will convict us when we sin, and even before we sin will try to convince us not to.

When He comes, He will convict *and* convince the world *and* bring demonstration to it about sin and about righteousness (uprightness of heart and right standing with God) and about judgment, John 16:8.The Holy Spirit will constantly highlight areas in our lives which we need change. If he never convicts, we will never be aware of where we are going wrong. Every time we yield to him during this process the more purified we will become. One may ask what the Holy Spirit uses in the likeness of water to sanctify us.

Sanctify them [purify, consecrate, separate them for Yourself, make them holy] by Truth, your word is Truth, John 17:17. In John 14:17 the Holy Spirit is called the Spirit of truth. The Spirit of truth is in the process of preparing the believers to spend eternity with the Christ. This preparation includes cleaning and purifying the lives of believers and enabling them to live holy. The Spirit of truth will sanctify, cleanse and make us holy by the truth which is enshrined in the Bible. Why has God chosen to sanctify us with truth rather than something else? Only the truth can expose a lie; falsehood, pretention, depravity and wickedness in our character and reveal our sins to us. It is only truth when applied will bring about purity and cleanliness. At different times the Holy Spirit will show us sinful habits in our lives in order to purge us of them but we must remain pure in that area of our life by abiding in the truth that was applied to make us clean, so that we may bear fruits of righteousness.

Truth is a preservative. The Holy Spirit does not only want us cleansed; he also wants to preserve us. When we purpose to walk in truth, the Spirit of Truth (Holy Spirit) himself will restrain and sustain us. This does not mean that the father of all lies, the devil, will not try to use people and situations in defiance of the truth to get us all dirty again. Consequently we should bear in mind that periods of testing will not destroy us but work to build faith and character in us. The Apostle Paul refers to these experiences as light momentary afflictions.

The Sacrifice of a Sweet Smelling Savor

The second aspect of Ruth's preparation was for her to anoint herself. This is not the kind of anointing that we ask God for, the anointing for which we ask is for service. Ruth was preparing for a date with destiny so she fragrant herself. Generally women love to fragrant themselves, particularly on special occasions. Similarly, believers are the bride of Christ, we are expected to make an even greater or decisive effort to ensure that our lives is as a sweet fragrance in the nostril of our God.

In the books of Exodus and Leviticus after God would have brought the children of Israel out of Egypt, he taught them how to make sacrifices to him. He told them what they should offer and how much, he told them how they should make the offering and the reason for each sacrifice. He did not leave it up to their imagination or discretion. Even though we no longer have to slaughter rams and bulls nor offer cakes to the Lord, we still need to offer sacrifices unto him every day of our life. We know from scripture what the necessities are so that as we surrender our life, a sacrificial offering to God we should so in the manner which he desires. "He has showed you, O man, what is good. And what does the Lord require of you? But to act justly and to love mercy and to walk humbly with your God", Micah 6:8. "And now O Israel, what does the Lord your God ask of you but to fear the Lord your God, to walk in all his ways, to love him, to serve the Lord your God with all your heart and with all your soul and to observe the Lord's commands and decrees that I am giving you today for your own good?" Deuteronomy 10:12&13

The other characteristic about the sacrifices offered was that they had to be burnt by fire before the sweet smelling aroma was released. Our sacrifices and offerings, which is our daily acts of life and service whether in the secular or spiritual arena will be treated as if burnt by fire. The purpose of fire is to test, consume and purify. God himself setting the flames, during the testing process that the impurities in our lives come to surface and are consumed. It is during the testing process that our motives for doing what we do will surface. God is not impressed with what we do or even how much we do but with what propels us to do it. When our motive for doing comes from a desire to please God and obey His word, when our sacrifices are being burnt by fires of criticisms, misrepresentations, delays, disappointments and hardships and when we are forced to venture out alone we will learn to stand importune and in faith. Preserved and strengthened in our spirit, we will not despair because our motive is right. Our sacrifices therefore will not be consumed because God will get the glory. However, when our motives are wrong, when the trials come, we will become frustrated, and will want to quit also. What we do will not last when we are seeking vain glory.

In order to preserve the integrity of our motive, the Lord Jesus taught us in Matthew 6:3, 4, 6 & 18, that when we give alms and charity, when we pray and fast we should do so in secret. The nugget revealed here could be applied to every area of our lives. And whilst we would not always be able to do everything in secret, the lesson here is we should not do what we do to impress others. Following this counsel will also cultivate in us a genuine and selfless character. At times, we will be forced into revealing what we do in secret because of the pressure of competitiveness around us, but we should never waste our time trying to prove or compare ourselves to anyone. This only serves to rob us of the greater reward.

Before fragrance can be released from our lives we must submit ourselves to the will of God. We must let go of our desires, our plans, our dreams, our will and our motives, so that God can burn, in the process of time, the carnal nature inside us. As our flesh metaphorically speaking, burns, there will be a stench. We all stink in one area or the other, bad reputation, bad attitudes, wrong motives, wicked ways, but as we willingly submit ourselves to be purified by fire on the altar, there will emanate from our lives a sweet smelling odour of a pure living sacrifice. This is what the Lord delights. This is what draws him to us. God does not have favourites but he will be drawn to those who deliberately perfumes for him.

Put on your Best Clothes

Ruth was still the woman seeking to find her place after her tragedy. In preparation for her change it was necessary for her to strip herself of the garments she wore. She had to bathe and perfume herself. Then put on her best clothes. The custom in Bible times and in some Middle Eastern countries is that, garments depict who you are; whether you are royalty, a virgin, married, widowed, or a harlot. What we wear today still speaks for us. But there is a lot of confusion for one can no longer easily tell a believer from a non-believer by mode of dress. Everyone seems to be caught up in the fashion explosion.

The scripture advises us as God's women how to dress. "I also want women to dress modestly, with decency and propriety, not with braided hair or gold or pearl or expensive clothes but with good deeds appropriate for women who profess to worship God," 1Timothy 2:9-10. Well, God helped me. I had a problem with this. Through my teenage years I dressed modestly. In fact I dressed so modestly that I almost broke the old fashion scale. However, in my early twenties I changed this manner of dress when I realized that I had the unique ability of making clothes look good. Particularly close fitting ones. I never wore short clothing or that which exposed areas that should be covered. But for me if it was tight then it was just right. I absolutely loved hanging my figure out. Almost every piece of clothes I owned was figure accentuating. I was not dressing in this manner to attract anyone; I did it for me. It made me happy. But later this manner of dressing became a source of intense struggle because I began to grow in my commitment to Christ and wanted to please Him. But I found it difficult to let go of my skinny clothing. In fact, it seemed as though I could not have won this battle regardless of how much I purposed in my heart to change this manner of dress. Every time I went shopping for clothing I found myself being drawn into purchasing close fitting clothing. One day I met a person and I remembered that person asking me, "Are you a Christian? Something about your mannerism tells me that you are, but when I look at you, girl, you are as hot as fire!" It was at this point that I came to myself and I recognized the level of confusion I was creating in the minds of people. I started to change the way I dressed. I shifted my focus from looking fabulous on the outside to being beautiful on the inside. I did not just look different; I felt different.

I believe that women should make every attempt to look beautiful. But in this attempt we must be careful that we do not beautify ourselves for the purpose of attracting men. Sometimes, our clothes preferences unfortunately attract the wrong men to us. In the spirit realm like spirits attract. Whenever we find that men are staring at us in a drooling manner, cat calling or are drawn to us in a sexual way, we should immediately recognize that this may be happening because of what we are wearing.

Women of God also need to remember that it is their responsibility to be their brother's keeper. One of the ways in which we achieve this goal is by dressing modestly. Women are not attracted to the opposite sex by what we see but rather through emotional stimulus. We may feel attracted to a man because he makes us feel admirable, secure, loved or cared for. Even acts of sexual intimacy are more emotional for women than they are physical. This is not the case with men. Men are stimulated and sexually drawn to a woman through the sight. For this reason Jesus spoke to men about looking at a woman to lust after her, Matthew 5:28. Because women are different it becomes difficult for them to understand the plight they put our brothers in when they wear certain types of clothing. They are blind to the fact that they sabotage and frustrate the efforts of our brothers who are still struggling to overcome the spirit of lust.

Some of you need to make adjustments in the way you dress bearing in mind that it is our responsibility to be our brother's keeper. Even as you make adjustments it may be a struggle at first, but do not give up. The fight is never over until we either win or give up. Even as we tread on the path to victory in this area of our lives I would suggest that we avoid shopping on impulse as this could lead us down the slope, slippery path again. With regards to the later portions of the scripture verses of 1 Timothy 2:9-10, I do not believe that the Apostle Paul was saying that we should not braid our hair or wear jewelry but he was guarding us against vain and excessive use.

What Is on Your spirit?

And it shall come to pass in the day of the LORD'S sacrifice, that he will punish the princes, and the king's children, and all such as are clothed with *strange apparel*, Zephaniah 1:8. The Prophet of God was talking to Israel about their manner of dress. He said that they were wearing strange apparel or heathen clothing. Israel had become polytheistic in their worship and began to offer sacrifices to other gods along with the Lord their God. We are then forced to ask ourselves what has sacrifice to do with clothing? The answer is everything. The children of Israel already had a unique manner of dressing which had set them apart in culture and worship. In honouring other gods the children of Israel had adopted the ways and customs of the people whose gods they worshipped.

The essence of sacrifice is to show honour and devotion both inwardly and outwardly. We know that we cannot serve God and the devil at the same time. In the same vein we cannot be honourable and devoted wives yet dress with the intentions of being physically appealing to other men. This is what Israel was trying to do, because of this when God looked at them he saw a people wearing strange apparel. They were no longer distinct in worship.

Like the children of Israel many believers are not distinct in worship. They put on and take off at will practices which they were distinctly told to put away. Their devotion has become divided and many have clothe their spirit with foul garments that they should not wear "But now put away and rid yourselves [completely] of all these things: anger, rage, bad feelings toward others, curses *and* slander and foulmouthed abuse and shameful utterances from your lips! Do not lie to one another...Colossians 3: 8-9. God has given us garments to clothe the entire inner man. Colossians 3:12 is one of the scriptures which instruct believers how to clothe their spirit. This portion of scripture says, "Since God chose you to be the holy people he loves, you must clothe yourself with tenderhearted mercy, kindness, humility, gentleness and patience."

CHAPTER FOUR

The Threshing Floor

Then Naomi her mother-in-law said to Ruth, My daughter, shall I not seek rest or a home for you, that you may prosper? And now is not Boaz, with whose maidens you were our relative? See, he is winnowing barley tonight at the threshing floor. Wash and anoint yourself therefore, and put on your best clothes and *go down to the threshing floor...* Ruth 3:1-3 (emphasis added)

Go Down to the Threshing Floor

*I*n Biblical times the manner of threshing grain consisted of two steps which served to separate grain from chaff. Firstly, the harvested stalks of grain were spread out on the threshing floor. Oxen or donkeys tied abreast were yoked to a threshing sledge then driven around several times over the stalks. Threshing could also be done by having oxen walk over the stalk or by beating them with sticks. This first process served to break the heads of grain from the stalks.

Secondly, the broken stalks were tossed into the air. The wind then blew the chaff to one side, while the grain fell into a pile on the floor to be gathered. The separation of grain from chaff by wind is called winnowing. Because wind was so vital to the process threshing floors were normally located in elevated areas such as hill tops and in large open fields. These floors were owned either by families or the entire village and often served as landmarks and meeting places. Threshing floors were so crucial to the life of the people that they were greatly valued but were often the object of attack whenever there was tribal rivalry. Thieves also raided threshing floors.

A Place of Separation and Transformation

The threshing floor is a place of separation and transformation. A harvest is useless unless it was processed on the threshing floor. During the reaping process harvesters were fully aware that only the grains were necessary yet they did not pluck these grains from the stalk. Instead they reaped the entire stalk, thus, gathering the good and bad, the wanted and unwanted. This was done because the harvesters did not only understood their role but they also knew that there was a process to follow which catered for this vital separation.

We are a harvest. We are the end result of all that we have been through, good and bad. But unlike a field of harvested grain, we were not all sown at the same time, we will not all become mature at the same time and pace, and the reality is some believers will never be sent down to the threshing floor because of their unwillingness to grow to that level of maturity in the Lord. However, believers who are growing in the grace and knowledge of our Lord and savior Jesus Christ will be sent down to the threshing floor.

It is through the threshing floor experiences, like the stalks of barley, the bad and unwanted stuff in and about us are be broken off and thrown away. When we first began our walk in Christ not all of our carnal mind-set, lifestyle or values was immediately taken away by the Holy Spirit. This is why we were able to get away with some things and in the midst of our blundering and stumbling he nourished and shielded us and placed people in our lives to hold us up in prayer. Had God dealt with us "tit for tat" every time we fell short, we would have all died in the field. He knows that we will grow to maturity, for we are his harvest and the threshing floor his process for development and change.

During our threshing process not everything that is broken off and crushed away is bad. Sometimes people are removed from our lives not because they are bad but because they were not assigned to take the journey with us in the next level of our walk. Some things are removed from our lives not because they are not good for us but because they are not necessary for where God is taking us. In the barley fields leaves, stalks and roots were necessary as these protected, nourished and supported the grains but are removed on the threshing floor because they are no longer needed. Sometimes both people and things are removed from our lives. This happens when God wants to teach us to stand alone, to deal with situations alone, and to learn to depend upon him alone. It is possible that we can become so dependent upon the people in our lives and upon our material acquisitions that we become independent of God. Therefore, it becomes necessary for God to thresh and winnow these things out our lives so that we can turn to him again, in total dependence.

Like any other processing the process of threshing was designed to produce change and development. This change elevates us spiritually, to know the presence of God, to tap into the power of God and to walk in the prosperity and blessings which God has ordained for those who serve him faithfully. However it is during this processing that thieves raid the threshing floor. The enemy will attempt to steal believer's faith through doubt, their confidence in God through double mindedness, their patience through anxiety, and their humility through pride. The enemy will use self pity to magnify the pain of the process thus causing some to walk away from the power and wisdom which comes from enduring much pain. The temptation to live a lie to impress others steals from us the freedom and expression pertaining to one's own life.

However those who allow themselves to be processed will progress. This progress is not to be measured according to the world's terms but according to God's standards and our relationship with him. When we choose to measure our personal progress by standards of the world system, we give them power over us; power to make us feel like a failure in the event that we are not attaining those things we perceive as success. On the other hand when we set our own standards even if we experience failure we can be free of the failure complex because we were not trying to live up to the expectations of others. Thus, we would be better equipped to use our failure as a springboard to leap over the hurdles of our set backs.

Progress entails embracing that which is unfamiliar, stepping into that which is new and making Godly connections to challenge and direct us. It is not always measured by the physical wealth we acquire. But whether measured by; material or spiritual concepts it is augmented by the relationship we have with God: our Heavenly Father, Jesus Christ, our redeemer, and the Holy Spirit by which we are sealed to the day of redemption. The God kind of progress is firstly about the wealth of God's grace and presence we possess or carry in our spirits. Our misguided minds sometimes force us to equate progress to physical wealth which men applaud as success but this is not always the case.

We live in an era where everyone wants to be a star, an idol or come into some sort of fame and fortune. It is like a flu that almost everyone is catching. God want His redeemed to prosper not just spiritually, but financially and in every other area of our lives. Psalm 35:27 tells us that God delights in the prosperity of His servants. But there are always criteria for progress and development. Seek God first; establish a balance life and a life of integrity before God and man. These principles open the way to privilege and access to material prosperity.

Trust and the Threshing Floor

It is easy to say that we trust God when things are going well in our lives. But the real test of trust comes when we are being threshed. As God strips us in places we never thought he would and he cuts and peels away from our lives things and people who are important to us. And situations which we never thought would have come our way, comes our way. While being threshed we will pray for breakthrough for weeks and months, sometimes years. While other get theirs we would not get ours. The threshing floor is not the place from which we would be able to manipulate God with our praise and worship or with fasting. And I know that folks tell us that if we fast and pray we would get our breakthrough but on the threshing floor that would not always be so, the truth is, we can only breakthrough after we would have come through our processing. During our processing we may encounter what seem like a series of unfortunate events. People would talk about us because of the troubles we are facing. Some would think that God is punishing us for some sin we committed. Some would disrespect us because they feel that God has abandoned us. It is only those who truly have our interest at heart would be able to stand and endure the processing with us. And it is sad to say that the great number of people we had buzzing around us during the good times would be greatly reduced to a faithful few. I, however, consider this a blessing because it enables us to identify those people whom we can truly rely on to stand with us in and through any situation.

Even with the faithful few by our sides offering their prayers and words of encouragement there are certain places in our trial that encouragement of people would not be as effective as it used to be. And some prayers would have to emerge from our spirits as silent travail in the secret places of our hearts because we do not want others to hear the questions we ask God. Because we were told it is not the Christian thing to do. Yet under pressure we confront God with questions not in arrogance or impatience but as a puzzled child questioning a father so as to gain greater clarity concerning issues at hand. And even if he does not respond we do not lose our confidence, but lay our petitions at his feet in absolute trust.

Trust is adamantly relying on God's obligation to be faithful to those who confidently rely on him. When we truly trust God we will grab a hold of victory by faith, because of our assurance of his faithfulness. We visualize ourselves not in our current situation but walking in that which God has promise because we are confident that he as able to do what he said he will do. And we will talk of victory even though we are surrounded by all the paraphernalia of a victim. Our confidence towards God would challenge us to agree with Job who testified of Him as one, "Who does great things past finding out", Job 9:10.

The threshing floor is a place where those who trust in God will emerge victorious. The use me, bless me but do not test me Christians would not be able to endure the trials of the threshing floor. I reiterate, not every believer will be sent down to the threshing floor and God will only allow us to go there when he know that we would be able to withstand the heat of its fire. For this reason we should not compare ourselves with others. We may want to look at another believer's life and question our self as to why they are going through all the troubles that they are encountering whilst we may not encounter such difficulties. We may even be tempted to think that something is wrong in their life when in fact they may have grown to a place of maturity in

God that we have not reached. And because of their maturity, God can allow them to be threshed for greater glory.

A Word of Instruction

"But when he lies down, notice the place where he lies; then go and uncover his feet and lie down. And he will tell you what to do", Ruth 3:4. When Ruth lay at Boaz feet, she risk losing her life. Boaz had no prior knowledge of her intention to approach him as redeemer. He could have responded in a harsh manner. Ruth, on the other hand, relied on his ability to be merciful and her desire was satisfied when Boaz responded with mercy. God is merciful towards us. When we rely on his mercy in our time of need it will be granted. Naomi was so confident that Boaz was going to deal mercifully with Ruth, that she told her, "he will tell you what to do". When we rely on God's ability to be merciful, we will approach him with confidence on every occasion. And in difficulties we will rest assured that God will tell us what to do. He will give us a word of instruction.

God has a word of instruction which will point us to the way out of the flames of our fiery trial. This would not be an issue of trial and error but a sure word from God loaded with power to seat and settle us into our place of rest. Victory lies in our willingness to obey that word of instruction which would be specific for each person and situation. Boaz's word of instruction to Ruth is stated in Ruth 3:11-13.

CHAPTER FIVE

The Encounter

Ruth approached quietly, uncovered his feet and lay down. In the middle of the night something startled the man, and he turned and discovered a woman lying at his feet. "Who are you?" he asked. "I am your servant Ruth," she said. *"Spread the corner of your garment over me,* since you are a kinsman redeemer."

Ruth 3:4-9

A Time to Grow

Healthy relationships grow. Ruth wanted the relationship between her and Boaz to grow from being that of casual acquaintances to the strength of a committed relationship. In order for this to happen she took the initiative, she voiced her desire. Like Ruth we should desire to experience a closer relationship with Jesus Christ and we should make deliberate efforts to ensure this happens.

In her quest to improve her relationship with Boaz, the scripture above records for us that Ruth laid down at Boaz's feet. She assumed a posture of submission. Submission is not a popular word nowadays. Everyone wants to stand up for themselves and let their voices be heard. But it is important that we understand that our place of submission is our place of power. Whoever we submit ourselves to we have access to their power. Since our focus is on fulfilling our God-given destinies it is important that we submit to God so that we may access his power to fulfill the purposes he has destined for us.

The word submission is made up of two words. Sub, the prefix implies that something or someone is beneath something or someone of greater authority or influence than itself. Mission the suffix implies an assignment or a representation in a foreign territory. As we embark on our mission to represent Jesus Christ in this foreign territory known as earth, it is necessary that we bring ourselves under his authority. This is best achieved through a closer relationship with him.

"*Later I passed by*, and when I looked at you and saw that you were old enough for love, I spread the corner of my garment over you and covered your nakedness. I gave you my solemn oath and entered into a covenant with you, declared the Sovereign Lord, and you became mine". Ezekiel 16:8.

"Later I passed by..." The love we had for the Lord at our initial salvation experience should grow over a period of time. Our initial love should grow to become mature love. God, through the Holy Spirit courts us so that we may fall more deeply in love with him. When we respond our love matures.

Mature love is not prompted into action it flows naturally. Many talk of love but have very little actions to support their words. Mature love is demonstrated in our worship, words and works. When we worship God in Spirit and Truth as he requires we become more like him. True worship transforms the worshiper into the image of Christ. A transformed person is Christlike in words and works. Thus, we need to measure ourselves alongside God's word in relation to our worship, words and works and see where we need to make adjustments so that we when the Lord pass by us he sees that we are old enough for love.

Covenants

Covenants are binding agreements which two parties knowingly enter into. Covenants should not be entered into hurriedly or unwisely as they must be kept faithfully and often throughout one's lifetime. Covenants made now affect generations to come.

People enter in covenantal agreement with each other for various reasons such as marriage, mutual protection, to secure peace, to commit to continued friendship, for promoting business and in order to secure assistance in time of war. However, people tend to shy away from entering into a covenant relationship with God because they are concerned about their ability to keep their part. However, God enables those who enter into such agreement with him to fulfill their obligations.

In the Old Testament there were several covenants. However, these covenants were between God and his chosen people Israel. Jesus Christ came and made a new and better covenant. Hebrew 7:22 and 8:7 testifies of this. When Jesus Christ made the new, better covenant he made it accessible to everyone. The Apostle Paul highlighted this in his letter to the gentile believers at Ephesus. "Therefore, remember that at one time you were Gentiles (heathens) in the flesh, call uncircumcision by those who called themselves circumcision, [itself a mere mark] in the flesh made by human hands. Remember that you were at one time separated (living apart) from Christ [excluded from all part in Him], utterly estranged and outlawed from the rights of Israel as a nation and strangers with no share in the sacred compacts of the [Messianic] promise [with no knowledge of or right in God's agreements, His covenants]. And you had no hope (no promise); you were in the world without God. But now in Christ Jesus, you who once were [so] far away, through (by, in) the blood of Christ have been brought near", Ephesians 2:11-13.

Jesus spoke of the new covenant as recorded in 1 Corinthians 11:25, "This cup is the new covenant between God and his people an agreement confirmed with my blood. Do this to remember me as often as you drink it." When the blood of Jesus Christ was shed on the cross of Calvary the way was opened for everyone to enter into a covenant as sacred and as unifying as marriage with him. Although everyone who has been redeemed has entered into this covenant relationship with Christ, only believers who are growing in their relationship with him will be able to relish in the blessings of this covenant relationship.

The Covenant of Marriage

Two similar statements were made at different times. "Spread the corner of your garment over me", Ruth 3:9. When Ruth made this statement, she was asking Boaz to marry her. She no longer wanted to be casually acquainted with this man. She wanted to be married to him. Thus, she made her desire known.

"I spread the corner of my garment over you" Ezekiel 16:8. God was declaring what he did when he saw that his people's love for him was maturing. They no longer wanted a casual relationship with him. Thus, he responded to their love by spreading the corner of his garment over them. This act signified that the Lord entered into a covenant as sacred and as unifying as marriage with his people.

A Mystery Revealed

The coming together of this foreign woman, Ruth and Boaz through redemption is a Biblical representation of the coming together which Christ Jesus desires to have with all mankind. Revelation 13:8 acknowledges Jesus Christ as the Lamb that was slain [in sacrifice] before the foundation of the world. Throughout the Old Testament we saw the redemptive love of Christ being extended as symbols and representations of that which was to come. Ephesians 5:30-32 unveils the coming together of husband and wife in marriage as the great mystery to which the relation of Christ and His Church are represented. This portion of scripture says, "For we are members of his body, of his flesh, and of his bones. For this cause shall a man leave his father and mother, and shall be joined unto his wife, and they two shall be one flesh. This is a great mystery: but I speak concerning Christ and the Church". The writer of Ephesians was talking about marriage between a man and a woman. Then, he went on to say it is a "mystery". A mystery is a secret that is well kept in plain sight or something that is not easily understood. So, what mystery was the writer talking about? I believe he was simply saying the union between man and woman is a visible, relatable representation of the oneness between Christ and those who belong to him, his Church. When we clearly understand this our mindsets will be completely transformed.

I am fully persuaded that for this reason Satan targets to destroy marriages between men and women by constantly strategizing new ways of infiltrating this sacred union. Satan also glamorizes personal independence and makes marital separation and divorce seem normal and acceptable. Further, he seeks to tarnish God's set standard of marriage between one man and one woman to same sex marriages and polygamous relationships. Satan knows if he is successful in destroying the visible, relatable representations of the sacred covenant relationship between God and his people his work to lead humanity astray will be much easier.

In Biblical times, particularly in the Old Testament the seriousness of cutting covenant was often witnessed by setting up a memorial as a sign to remind the parties involved of the covenant they made with each other. This was done through setting up stone altars as in the case of Jacob and Laban. Some exchanged their garments, in the case of David and Jonathan.

In our day, newlyweds exchange wedding bands as a sign of their entering into covenant with each other. As with marriage between a man and a woman, there are many similar symbolism of our coming together as one with Jesus Christ.

Vows

The consensus of union requires the joining and coming together of separate parts to make a whole. The hallmark of the covenant of marriage is the joining together of two hearts, thus making them one. When a couple marries they commit themselves to each other by making vows.

People come into a union with Christ through confession and belief. "Because if you acknowledge and confess with your lips that Jesus is Lord and in your heart believe (adhere to, trust in, and rely on the truth) that God raised Him from the dead, you will be saved. For with the heart a person believes (adheres to, trusts in, and relies on Christ) and is so justified (declared righteous, acceptable to God), and with the mouth he confesses (declares openly and speaks out freely his faith) and confirms [his] salvation." Romans 10:9-10

Christ made this promise to his people. "And I will betroth you to me forever; yes, I will betroth you to me in righteousness and justice, in steadfast love and in mercy. I will even betroth you to me in stability *and* in faithfulness, and you shall know (recognize, be acquainted with, appreciate, give heed to, and cherish) the Lord." Hosea 2:19,20.

Covenant Meal

Newlyweds feed each other with wine and cake on their wedding day. Jesus shared a covenant meal of bread and wine with His disciples on the night in which He was betrayed. The meal was very significant to him, his disciples and to us. Through this meal Jesus instituted the new covenant. The sharing of a covenant meal signifies that those who enter into such an agreement will be sharing as one everything which is to come. Jesus is always present no matter what we go through.

Whosoever decides to enter into a covenant relationship with Jesus Christ can partake of this covenant meal. In fact Jesus told his disciples "Do this to remember me". Those redeemed by his blood are also to partake of this covenant meal we know as communion. When we participate in this meal we are acknowledging, reaffirming and celebrating the fact that we are delivered from sin and death and we can now experience abundant life through a new covenant.

There are blessings to be received by those who keep their part of covenant and curses for covenant breakers. 1 Corinthians 11:27-30 say "So anyone who eats this bread or drinks this cup of the Lord unworthily is guilty of sinning against the body and blood of the Lord. This is why you should examine yourself before eating the bread and drinking the cup. For if you eat the bread or drink the cup without honoring the body of Christ you are eating and drinking God's judgment upon yourself. This is why many of you are weak and sick and some have even died."

My Ishi.

Before I continue I will make a cursory pause to say this. God is spirit. He is neither male nor female. However, through figurative language referred to as anthropomorphism human characteristics are assigned to God. Thus, in scriptures we see God being referred to as father Romans 8:15, bridegroom Mark 2:19, and husband Jeremiah 31:32. God chose to reveal himself to us through the use of masculine titles. However, this does not grant us permission to limit God to a gender, rather the use of these terms help us to relate to and communicate with God.

"And it shall be in that day, says the Lord, that you shall call Me Ishi [my husband], and you shall no more call me Baali [my Baal]," Hosea 2:16. Jesus is as a husband to everyone who is redeemed. Out of this covenant relationship as husband he provides, protects, heals, delivers, defends and do all of the other things he does for us. He also keeps his promises, and he remains faithful to us. He is our husband. Ishi is the husband name of Christ. In that day when we clearly understand and acknowledge Christ as our husband we will be able to effectively experience the tangible manifestations of the power, privilege and possibilities that is associated with this type of relationship.

The Union is Legal

Marriages are only recognized as lawful when the legal requirements are adhered to. One of the legal requirements of a marriage is that the transaction must be done in the presence of witnesses.

Boaz made the transaction of the redemption of Ruth legal. "Now formerly in Israel this was the custom concerning redeeming and exchanging. To confirm a transaction, a man pulled off his sandal and gave it to the other. This was the way of attesting in Israel. Therefore, when the kinsman said to Boaz, buy it for yourself, he pulled off his sandal. And Boaz said to the elders and to all the people, you are witnesses this day that I have bought all that was Eleminech's and all that was Chilion's and Mahlon's from the hand of Naomi. Also Ruth the Moabitess, the widow of Mahlon, I have bought to be my wife to restore the name of the dead to his inheritance that the name of the dead may not be cut off from among his brethren and from the gate of his birthplace. You are witnesses this day." Ruth 4:7-10.

Jesus made the transaction of the redemption of mankind legal. "Having cancelled *and* blotted out *and* wiped away the handwriting of the note (bond) its legal decrees *and* demands which was in force *and* stood against us (hostile to us). This [note with its regulations, decrees, *and* demands] He set aside *and* cleared completely out of our way by nailing it to [His] cross. [God] disarmed the principalities and powers that were ranged against us and made a bold display *and* public example of them, in triumphing over them in Him and in it [the cross]". Colossians 2:14-15

Surnamed

When a woman marries she is surnamed by her husband. This change in name symbolizes a common identity and stands as a public testimony of the union. The sharing of the same name lets the world know that the couple is a part of each other whilst also granting them the rights, privilege, power and authority to act as representatives of each other whenever it becomes necessary.

All those who are redeemed are surnamed by Christ. "For the sake of Jacob My servant and of Israel My chosen, I have called you by your name. I have surnamed you, though you have not known Me." Isaiah 45:4.God said these words to his people. God expects us to use his name.

Although we humble ourselves to Christ and functions as servants, when we use the name of Jesus we are not using this name as mere servants. Rather, we are using the name of Jesus as someone who is in a covenant relationship that is as unifying as marriage. We have the privilege, power, authority and access to use the name of Jesus because we are surnamed. Consequently, when we use the name of Jesus to speak to principalities and powers, rulers of darkness and adversity, situations must respond in accordance to our command.

Jesus is expecting us to use his name, act on his behalf, function and live like him in the earth. Further, he is expecting us to use his name to conduct legal transactions so that his will and rule is manifested in the earth as it is in heaven. Jesus made this truth known in Matthew 16:19, "I will give you the keys of the kingdom of heaven, and whatever you bind on earth shall be bound in heaven, and whatever you loose on earth shall be loose in heaven."

Divine Alignment through Covenant

So Boaz took Ruth and she became his wife. Then he went to her, and the Lord enabled her to conceive, and she gave birth to a son. Then the women said to Naomi: "Praise be to the Lord, who this day has not left you without a kinsman-redeemer. May he become famous throughout Israel! He will renew your life and sustain you in your old age. For your daughter-in-law, who loves you and who is better to you than seven sons have given birth. Then Naomi took the child, laid him in her lap and cared for him. The women living there said, "Naomi has a son." And they named him Obed. He was the father of Jesse, the father of David, [the ancestor of Jesus Christ] Ruth 4:13- 17.

Ruth's story commenced with sadness and sorrow but concluded with gladness and joy. Not only did she experience redemption and restoration but the person connected to her, Naomi was also able to experience restoration. Everything which was out of order in Ruth's life through her pain and her past was realigned through her marriage to Boaz. Thus she was empowered and enabled to fulfill the purpose for which she was born.

Hosea 2:20-22 says, "I will be faithful to you and make you mine, and you will finally know me as the Lord. In that day I will answer says the Lord. I will answer the sky as it pleas for clouds. And the sky will answer the earth with rain. Then the earth will answer the thirsty cries of the grain, the grapevines and the olive trees. And they in turn will answer Jezreel-God plants." This scripture speaks of divine alignment. Our lives may have commenced or had been punctuated with sadness and sorrow but we can conclude our story with joy and fulfillment because we are in covenant with Christ. Through this relationship we are divinely aligned to access whatever we need to live a fulfilling life, and we are empowered and enabled to fulfill the destinies for which we were born.